THERE IS A SPIRIT

The Nayler Sonnets

BY

KENNETH BOULDING

FELLOWSHIP PUBLICATIONS

NYACK, NEW YORK

SIXTH PRINTING, 1964

*Set by hand at
The Golden Hind Press
Madison, New Jersey*

FOREWORD

IN Steig's collection of cartoons called *The Lonely Ones* all the well known behavior patterns of our time are treated. One of these, and not the least funny, is of a man self-tied into knots with the caption "I solve all my difficulties by meditation."

Yes, the world now knows there is a specific reaction called meditation. But, knowing no more, it can only laugh, as, one hundred years ago, Charles Dickens laughed at the students of Pre-Raphaelite art. Dickens thought Giotto an old fool who could not paint, and those who studied him frauds and escapists from the art and discipline of painting. There are Pre-Raphaelites now in religion—those who are determined by study and method to recapture a lost secret. Meditation is nearly as bad a word as Pre-Raphaelitism but, even more certainly, it does stand for a method.

This may seem a queer introduction to any sonnet sequence, but it is not to these sonnets on James Nayler by Kenneth Boulding. As the poet says, they are a "purely personal act of meditation." They expand into memorable form the last words of Nayler as he lay dying and expressed a faith which had carried him from the early fevers of evangelism through extremities of brutal torture and contempt to death by violence.

These sonnets, then, are not art forms but technics. They are beautiful but in the right way—when aesthetic pleasure is an overtone experienced as the soul realizes an extension of insight. Why use poetry? is a pre-psychological question answered briefly by the technical phrase "affirmational meditation." Skilled and fitting phrases—sentences so well shaped that they will bear much repetition and carry intellectual and emotional sense—are necessary for deep meditation. English poetry is superb but, sadly, almost entirely confines its meditation to human love and beauty, not to divine. Mr. Boulding's sonnets are then beautifully made "spiritual exercises." They may also, one hopes, be the first swallows of a new summer of our poetry, a summer lit not by the human but by the Divine Sun.

GERALD HEARD

CONTENTS

INTRODUCTION

JAMES NAYLER was born near Wakefield, in Yorkshire, England, about the year 1616. He fought in Cromwell's army against the Scots, and afterwards became a powerful preacher and one of the early leaders of the Society of Friends. "I was struck with more terror by the preaching of James Nayler, than I was at the battle of Dunbar" wrote James Gough, another early Friend. In 1656 he was led into certain excesses of conduct by the hysterical enthusiasm of some of his followers, and allowed himself to be led into Bristol on a horse while his followers strewed garments in the way and shouted "Holy, holy, holy, Lord God of Sabaoth." For this blasphemy, as it was considered, he was cruelly punished by an illegal action of parliament, being severely whipped, branded with the letter B on his forehead, and having his tongue bored through with a red hot iron. After this punishment he was imprisoned in one of the horrible "holes" of the time, but he recovered his judgment, was eventually reconciled with Friends and came to condemn his previous behavior. He was released from prison in September 1659. In October 1660 he set off from London northwards on foot, intending to visit his wife and children in Wakefield. On the way he was robbed, and found bound in a field. He was taken to a Friend's house, where he died. The passage which forms the basis of these sonnets was spoken by him about two hours before his death. It is a classic expression of a spirit too close to the source of truth to have a name. It deserves to be read slowly, and deeply, so that its truth will burn through the plausible lies which form the principal furniture of our minds. It carries a message of peace to a world at war, a clear wind of pure truth amid the fogs of propaganda and deceit, an intimation of that love which is indeed God. There are times and places in history when we feel the wings of the spirit brushing very close to earth. The tragedy of James Nayler is such an occasion. Even while we cannot approve the pitiful and absurd behavior of his followers, yet we can agree with them in this: that here we are close indeed to the spirit of Christ.

I have written these sonnets, partly as a purely personal act of meditation and devotion, but partly also in the hope that they may call the attention of others to the depths of truth in the passage which fathered them. It may be wondered why in this age of free (and occasionally easy) verse anyone should bother to compress his thought into the archaic straight-jacket of the conventional sonnet. Nevertheless, as metal must be run into a tight mold before it can become a bell, so the intellectual and aesthetic effort required to compress an explosive idea into the formal limits of a sonnet may cause the truth within the words to ring all the more clearly. Every one of Nayler's phrases is packed with significance, and the attempt both to expand and extract this significance, and to compress it into the sonnet form has been a joyful and illuminating spiritual experience for me. I dare not hope that the sonnets can convey much of this experience to others. I can hope, however, that they may lead others to dig in the same mines of truth.

THERE IS A SPIRIT WHICH I FEEL that delights to do no evil, nor to revenge any wrong, but delights to endure all things, in hope to enjoy its own in the end. Its hope is to outlive all wrath and contention, and to weary out all exaltation and cruelty, or whatever is of a nature contrary to itself. It sees to the end of all temptations. As it bears no evil in itself, so it conceives none in thoughts to any other. If it be betrayed, it bears it, for its ground and spring is the mercies and forgiveness of God. Its crown is meekness, its life is everlasting love unfeigned; and takes its kingdom with entreaty and not with contention, and keeps it by lowliness of mind. In God alone it can rejoice, though none else regard it, or can own its life. It's conceived in sorrow, and brought forth without any to pity it, nor doth it murmur at grief and oppression. It never rejoiceth but through sufferings: for with the world's joy it is murdered. I found it alone, being forsaken. I have fellowship therein with them who lived in dens and desolate places in the earth, who through death obtained this resurrection and eternal holy life.

JAMES NAYLER

1660

· X ·

THE NAYLER SONNETS

1. *There is a spirit which I feel*

CAN I, imprisoned, body-bounded, touch
The starry robe of God, and from my soul,
My tiny Part, reach forth to his great Whole,
And spread my Little to the infinite Much,
When Truth forever slips from out my clutch,
And what I take indeed, I do but dole
In cupfuls from a rimless ocean-bowl
That holds a million million million such?

And yet, some Thing that moves among the stars,
And holds the cosmos in a web of law,
Moves too in me: a hunger, a quick thaw
Of soul that liquefies the ancient bars,
As I, a member of creation, sing
The burning oneness binding everything.

11. *That delights to do no evil*

SHALL I be good because of some reward,
   Because the virtuous act pays dividends
   In candy bars, the approving nods of friends,
In many tongues to praise, and hands to applaud,
In riches, honors, lavishly outpoured?
Or, since to ruin all things earthly tend,
Shall I be good to gain the greatest end,
The crown of bliss that Heaven may afford?

    Ask the sweet spring upon the mountain top
    What makes his sinless water flow so free:
    Is it the call of some far-distant sea,
    Or the deep pressure that no crust can stop?
    No conscious end can drag us out of sin,
    Unless clear goodness wells up from within.

III. *Nor to revenge any wrong*

NOW am I veined by an eroding doubt,
Insidious as decay, with poison rife.
Is love indeed the end and law of life,
When lush, grimacing hates so quickly sprout?
I thought in ignorance I had cast out
The sneaking devils of continuing strife,
But as the cancer thwarts the surgeon's knife,
So does revenge my sword of reason flout.

But though hate rises in enfolding flame
At each renewed oppression, soon it dies;
It sinks as quickly as we saw it rise,
While love's small constant light burns still the same.
Know this: though love is weak and hate is strong,
Yet hate is short, and love is very long.

IV. *But delights to endure all things*

HOW to endure, when all around us die
  Nations and gracious cities, homes and men,
  And the sweet earth is made a filthy den
Beneath whose roof black, belching vultures fly:
How to endure the darkness, when the sky
Is totally eclipsed by evil, when
Foul grinning Chaos spreads its reign again
And all good things in senseless ruin lie.

  Must we be hard as stone? It wears to dust.
  As stiff as oaks? But they untimely break.
  As pitiless as steel? It turns to rust,
  And Time from Pyramids will ruins make.
  In violence, decay, starvation, need,
  What can endure? Only the living Seed.

v. *In hope to enjoy its own in the end*

SMALL flowers there are beside the stoniest way,
  And on the seeming-endless journeying
  Some breaths of air are sweet, and some birds sing,
And some new goal is reached in every day;
Yet for the unknown end we wait and pray,
When the last knot of this world's tangled string
Is straightened out, and every evil thing
Redeemed in heaven's undisputed sway.

    We know not how the day is to be born,
    Whether in clouds of glory, tongues of flame,
    As once at Pentecost the Spirit came,
    Or whether imperceptibly as dawn;
    But as the seed must grow into the tree,
    So life is love, and love the end must be.

WHO weeps for Babylon, who mourns for Tyre,
Who worships proud imperious Caesar now?
The wreath, woven to fit a tyrant's brow
So soon is trampled in oblivion's mire.
Buried the ash of Moloch's dreadful fire,
Withered and lost Astarte's golden bough,
And turned beneath the lonely peasant's plough
Lie splintered shards of heathen altars dire.

Victorious lava sears the mountain side,
And leaves a cicatrice among the green,
But sun and frost and rain, and roots unseen
Advance the slow, resistless verdant tide.
Through all events runs one repeating rule,
That life may grow, but wrath and hatred cool.

VII. *And to weary out all exaltation and cruelty*

WHAT patience must we cherish, to out-wear
The sleepless hosts of hell, who lie in wait
Against our slightest weakness, early, late,
With perseverance more than we can bear.
How can we wait the many a weary year
Before the rock of pride, and cruel hate,
Into a fruitful earth disintegrate
Under the tears of love and near-despair?
Who then can blame us if we lose our trust
In Love's slow ways, and hastily rush to blast
The rock to pieces—but to find at last
When smoke has cleared, not earth, but barren dust.
Only by endless rain the soil is given,
And endless patience is the way of Heaven.

VIII. *Or whatever is of a nature contrary to itself*

IF GOD be All in All, must all be good?
    What then of evil?—of the shriek in the night,
    The slavering jaw, the glinting eye, the plight
Of mouse, fawn, coney? If this mystery could
By some veil-rending flash be understood,
Would Darkness shine with its own holy light,
Wrong but reflect the under-side of Right,
And Life exult beneath Death's sheltering hood?
        Are there no contraries at the heart of things?
        The double thread winds deep, beyond the reach
        Even of faith's white beam: and whether breach
        Or union comes at last, no prophet sings.
        Yet—if in this life love can weary out
        The staunchest evil: does God lie in doubt?

IX. *It sees to the end of all temptations*

WHAT is the end of greed but emptiness,
And what the end of a determined lust
But staleness, unfulfillment, sick disgust,
A debt of pride unpaid, and no redress?
Always we give the more, and gain the less
In bargaining with the ambassadors of dust:
Who, knowingly, would rate their contract just—
Ten future "No's" for one sweet present "Yes"!
Need we but sight to run from every shame,
The sight that sees the future opened bare?
Or does a doom, writ with a darker name,
Condemn us to a tunnel of despair?
Not sight alone, but Will, by love made free
Can make us walk the pilgrim way we see.

x. *As it bears no evil in itself*

IF SOUL be soil what may not grow therein?
  The indifferent ground cares not what plant it feed;
  Both the good grain and the lean poisoned weed
Out of its fecund womb their life may win.
Can there then be a soil that grows no sin,
That nourishes no thought of pride or greed,
And bears no plant not fruiting for the need
Of the good gardener and his humble kin?

      Not in man's world, where saviors do not save;
      Where painless, glib goodwill for humankind
      Serves but to rub the sores it cannot bind,
      And Liberators leave man more a slave;
      But out of harrowed heart and broken will
      Ground is prepared at last that grows no ill.

XI. *So it conceives none in thoughts to any other*

IS THERE indeed a river that can clean
The stable of my thought? Can I not hide,
Behind the glittering wall of outward pride
In virtuous act, the dismal inward scene?
Not what we think, but what we do has been
The standard of the world: so have I tried
To wall out God with deeds. And yet inside
My soul blazes His light despite my screen.

Ah! Blinding Union! Now falls away
The shelly life of outward righteousness.
Torrential seas of brightness round me press,
Turning my secret night to open day,
Till in the fullness of Thy light no room
Is left for any cherished walléd gloom.

XII. *If it be betrayed, it bears it*

IT IS not hard to turn the other cheek
     After an insult, or hot tempered blow,
     And easier still it is, if we but know
How deadly are the weapons of the meek:
But treachery! That's evil at its peak,
Not to be suffered: easier far to go
The second mile with enemies, than show
Love to deceitful friends—Faugh! how they reek
Of cowardice, and the stale grey stench of fear!
Can I bear this, and bear it to the end?
     Yet, Lord, do I not name myself Thy friend,
     And then betray Thee oft, with word or sneer
     Or silence—and Thou bearest it, content
     To wait in long love on my betterment.

XIII. *For its ground and spring is the mercies and forgiveness of God*

MY LORD, Thou art in every breath I take,
And every bite and sup taste firm of Thee.
With buoyant mercy Thou enfoldest me,
And holdest up my foot each step I make.
Thy touch is all around me when I wake,
Thy sound I hear, and by Thy light I see
The world is fresh with Thy divinity
And all Thy creatures flourish for Thy sake.

    For I have looked upon a little child
    And seen Forgiveness, and have seen the day
    With eastern fire cleanse the foul night away;
    So cleansest Thou this House I have defiled.
    And if I should be merciful, I know
    It is Thy mercy, Lord, in overflow.

XIV. *Its crown is meekness*

HOW every virtue casts a mimic shade
  Of subtle vice, so like in form and face
  That shadow oft usurps the royal place
Of substance, in unholy masquerade.
So rotten pride, in pity's garb arrayed,
Drops hidden poison in the springs of grace,
And selfishness transmutes to metal base
The gold of love, by lesser love betrayed.
    But most of all, the very crown of good,
    Unconquerable Meekness, is pursued
    By the grey ghost compliance, bland and lewd,
    And cowardice seeks to stand where courage stood.
    Yet no deceit of words can hide for long
    The seed of life, the meekness of the strong.

XV. *Its life is everlasting love unfeigned*

CAUGHT in a mirrored maze of bright deceit,
    Peopled with images, that but reflect
    The groping movements of the intellect,
Till bounds are smudged where fact and shadow meet,
The mind is lost, until with quickened beat
Love scents a wind, blowing from God, unchecked,
And senses, deeper laid than sight, direct
To the free air our once-bewildered feet.
    But love must be made pure to be our guide;
    Not trader's love, that seeks more in return,
    But love that with clear, slender flame will burn
Though it be spent for nought, spurned, crucified,
    Until to one vast song our spirit lifts:
    To love for Love alone, not for His gifts.

XVI. *And takes its kingdom with entreaty and not with contention*

ARE there no armies, no angelic hosts,
  Invincibly arrayed in awful might,
  To battle with the shapeless forms of night,
The slimy writhing ranks that Satan boasts?
Has Heaven no navies to assault the coasts
Of Hell's hard Kingdom, cliffed with vulcanite?
Can Hell be taken with thin wisps of light,
Handwringing, cooing, pale, entreating ghosts?

    What Kingdom yet has been by wooing won?
    What King for words has willed his crown away?
    Then with what right of reason dost thou say
    Thou hast a Kingdom where there can be none?
    Ah!—but what know ye, ye blind lords of strife,
    About the secret Kingdom of Man's life!

XVII. *And keeps it by lowliness of mind*

NO KINGDOM falls before it is betrayed
By inward enemies—no outward foe
Can deal the last, and only fatal blow
That turns defeat to death. So am I preyed
Upon by subtle fears, lest I have laid
Thy kingdom in me open to a slow
Unseen decay that yet may bring it low,
And desolate the joy that Thou hast made.

For see—the stony citadel of pride,
My inmost stronghold, is rebellious still
Against the peaceful envoys of Thy will.
Ah, Lord, run through me with Thy sudden tide,
For this proud heart can never be Thy throne
Unless its pride be pride of Thee alone.

XVIII. *In God alone it can rejoice*

I PLUNGE me, shouting, in the fecund tide
 Of vast creation; lave myself in light,
 Dwell with imperial clouds, cloak with the night,
And woo the earth as lover woos a bride;
Through intricate kingdoms of pure sound I ride
On music, and on laughter, and invite
My joyful body-spirit to unite
With scent, taste, touch: all senses sanctified.
    What then! In God alone I must rejoice?
    Not in His creatures, His abounding gifts?
    The veil of sensual goodness lightly lifts
    And through the inward seam there drops a voice:
    "Could any gift its giver's loss atone,
    Or joy be sure, except its source be known?"

XIX. *Though none else regard it, or can own its life*

ARE not my friends built round me like a wall?
　　We stand together in a firm stockade
　　Around the cheerful fire our faith has made,
Its light reflected from the eyes of all.
Beyond the glow, in night's unechoing hall
Slide shadows, hideous offspring of the shade
Of unacknowledged doubt—but who's afraid
Of spectres, when there's fire, and friends at call?
　　But ah!—let death, or faithlessness, or doubt
　　Pluck out the stakes of this protecting fence
　　And leave me shivering in the bleak, immense,
　　Dark Otherness—will not my fire go out?
　　Our gathered sticks are scattered: but the sun
　　Warms many no more certainly than one.

xx. *It's conceived in sorrow, and brought forth without any to pity it*

MUST every flower reek of its mother dung,
    And every joy spring rash from beds of pain?
    Must every bliss be minted with a bane,
And songs of joy to mournful chants be sung?
What though the saints from misery's mass have wrung
Their drops of living water—can the chain
Of golden love the pearl of price sustain
When all the weight of woe thereon is hung?
    Lord, could'st Thou not have bought this life of Thine
    That we inherit, at a cost less great?
    Was there no way to Thee, no other gate
    But sorrow's gloomy cave, where no lights shine
    But Thy small rush? Then did'st Thou give us night
    For stars, and give us suffering for Thy light?

XXI. *Nor doth it murmur at grief and oppression*

MUST Christian Love move us to fat content
With the black dismal mass of man's distress?
And wrapped in God, must we then blandly bless
Wretchedness, pain, disease, as Heaven-sent
To prove our virtue, channel our intent
Away from Earth, where power and lust oppress
The ancient-suffering seed of gentleness,
And wealth and health always for nought are spent?
    Ah, never, never! If this thing were true,
    That we are cattle, tortured, that God's grace
    May shine: I would deny Him to His face.
    And yet—and yet—if God should suffer too,
    And share, and love, and die: may we not see
    The paradox . . . blaze into Mystery?

XXII. *It never rejoiceth but through sufferings*

CAN grief be gift, love's gift, Divine Love's gift?
    Not gentle grief over imagined loss,
    But vital-tearing agonies, that toss
All bodily organs into a bottomless pit
Of choking pain? Ah, dare we, dare we sift
The abyss of suffering, truly take our cross
To the insane pit of pain, and there emboss
Love's symbol on a door Hope cannot lift?

    Thou sayest it—and yet the very tongue
    That mouthed these words was bored with blackening
        flame,
    Seared with twice-bitter tasting pain and shame.
    No greater song than this the saints have sung:
    That there is joy, greater than Joy can know,
    Through suffering, on the far side of woe.

XXIII. *For with the world's joy it is murdered*

I WILL not shout for victory, nor praise
   The bloody laurels of returning hosts
   Above the throaty cries I conjure ghosts
Of slain to pave the ceremonial ways.
And neither will I mourn defeated days,
When the stiff pomp that martial grandeur boasts
Cracks into chaos on forsaken coasts,
And the bald, craven head is stripped of bays.
      Not with the world's joy will I raise my heart,
      Nor with the world's grief bow it down to dust;
      I will not sell it in an earthly mart,
      For every earthly love is kin to lust.
      The living soul must find securer worth
      In grief of Heaven than in joy of earth.

XXIV. *I found it alone, being forsaken*

THERE is no death but this, to be alone,
        Outside the friendly room of time and space,
        Forsaken by the comfortable face
Of things familiar, human, measured, known.
Not in raw fires, nor in the imagined groan
Of tortured body-spirits, do we trace
The shape of Hell; but in that dreadful place
Where in the vision nought but self is shown.

        And yet—he found it there, as on the cross
        When even God had fled, Love did not die:
        So from the last despair, the extremest cry,
        Flows the great gain that swallows all our loss.
        And from the towers of Heaven calls the bell
        That summons us across the gulf of Hell.

xxv. *I had fellowship therein with them who lived in dens and desolate places in the earth*

CAN I have fellowship with them that fed
　　On desert locusts, or the husks of swine,
　　Slept without tent, went naked as a sign,
And made the unforgiving earth their bed?
When I in gentle raiment have been led
Through pastures green, and have sat down to dine
At banquets, and have let my limbs recline
On easy couches, and slept comforted?

　　How can we pray for daily bread, with lip
　　Still smacking from a comfortable meal,
　　Or how, from Dives lofty table feel
　　With Lazarus the glow of fellowship,
　　Unless, with spirits destitute, we find
　　Fellowship in the deserts of the mind.